MAN-MADE HORRORS

BY JOHN HAMILTON

VISIT US AT
WWW.ABDOPUBLISHING.COM

Published by ABDO Publishing Company, 4940 Viking Drive, Suite 622, Edina, Minnesota 55435.
Copyright ©2007 by Abdo Consulting Group, Inc. International copyrights reserved in all countries.
No part of this book may be reproduced in any form without written permission from the publisher.
ABDO & Daughters™ is a trademark and logo of ABDO Publishing Company.

Printed in the United States.

Editor: Jim Ollhoff
Graphic Design: Sue Hamilton
Cover Design: Neil Klinepier
Cover Illustration: Corbis
Interior Photos and Illustrations: p 1 Godzilla vs Mecha-Godzilla, AP/Wideworld; pp 4-5 *Frankenstein*, courtesy Universal Pictures; p 6 *Frankenstein* poster, courtesy Universal Pictures; p 7 Mary Shelley, Corbis; p 8 Boris Karloff, courtesy Universal Pictures; p 9 Colin Clive, courtesy Universal Pictures; p 10 Robby the Robot, Corbis; p 11 R2-D2 & C3PO, Getty; p 12 *Blade Runner*, Corbis; p 13 Will Smith, Getty; p 14 *Eight Legged Freaks* poster & images, courtesy Warner Bros. Pictures; p 15 (top) *Godzilla King of the Monsters!*, courtesy Embassy Pictures Corp.; (bottom) *Godzilla* (1998), courtesy TriStar Pictures; p 16 (top) *Jurassic Park III* still, Corbis; (bottom) *Jurassic Park* (book), courtesy Alfred A. Knopf, Inc.; p 17 (top) *Resident Evil 2*, courtesy Capcom; (bottom) *Doom* still, courtesy Universal Pictures; p 18 (left) *A Sound of Thunder*, courtesy Warner Bros. Pictures; (right) *Timecop*, courtesy Universal Pictures; p 19 Ray Bradbury, AP/Wideworld; p 20 Arnold Schwarzenegger Terminator wax model, Getty; p 21 Terminator Robot, Corbis; p 22 *Dr. Jekyll and Mr. Hyde* picture still and poster, courtesy Paramount Pictures; p 23 Robert Louis Stevenson, Corbis; p 24 *Freddy vs. Jason*, courtesy New Line Cinema; p 25 John Carpenter, Corbis; p 26 Newspaper 1888, Getty; p 27 London street, Getty; p 28 Chernobyl victim monument, AP/Wideworld; p 29 (top) Smoggy Los Angeles, Getty; (middle) Toyota Prius, Getty; (bottom) Plastic recycling plant, Getty; p 31 Steven Spielberg, Corbis; p 32 *The Phantom Creeps*, courtesy Universal Pictures

Library of Congress Cataloging-in-Publication Data

Hamilton, John, 1959-
  Man-made horrors / John Hamilton.
     p. cm. -- (The world of horror)
  Includes index.
  ISBN-13: 978-1-59928-769-0
  ISBN-10: 1-59928-769-2
  1. Horror tales, English--History and criticism--Juvenile literature. 2. Science fiction, English--History and criticism--Juvenile literature. 3. Shelley, Mary Wollstonecraft, 1797-1851. Frankenstein--Juvenile literature. 4. Stevenson, Robert Louis, 1850-1894. Strange case of Dr. Jekyll and Mr. Hyde--Juvenile literature. 5. Monsters in literature--Juvenile literature. 6. Monsters in motion pictures--Juvenile literature. 7. Robots in literature--Juvenile literature. 8. Robots in motion pictures--Juvenile literature. I. Title.

PR830.T3H36 2007
823'.0873809--dc22
                                2006032727

CONTENTS

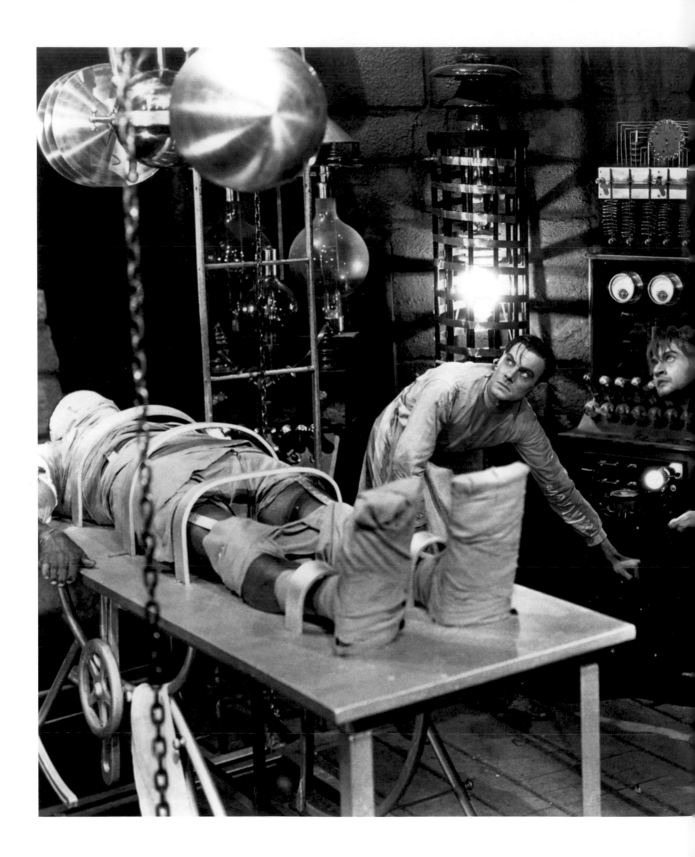

IT'S ALIVE! ALIVE!

With those fateful words, Dr. Victor Frankenstein announced to the world an achievement that he had created with his own two hands. By virtue of his science, his technology, and his own ego, he had brought something to life. But he would later regret it.

Man-made horrors are the problems that we create for ourselves. They might be experiments gone wrong, robots that run amok, or technology that is out of control. Unlike vampires, werewolves, or angry aliens, man-made horrors are not thrust upon us by an outside force. Man-made horrors are disasters that we do to ourselves.

These kinds of horror stories are popular because they have an element of truth to them. Which is easier to believe: angry space aliens wanting to destroy our planet, or human scientists making terrible mistakes? It's more fun to believe in space aliens, but it's a lot easier to believe greedy scientists making mistakes—and that's what man-made horror stories are all about.

Many of the stories of man-made horror struggle with questions like, "what is life?" and "when does life start?" Good stories help us think through these difficult questions.

Other stories of man-made horror are warnings. They warn that science and technology can make life better, but they can also make life much worse. Some stories of man-made horror tell of scientists who make mistakes because of their overconfidence, or because they use technology for the wrong reasons. As horror fiction warns us, science, technology, and nature can quickly get out of control.

Left: A scene from 1931's *Frankenstein,* a story of a scientist attempting to create life.

FRANKENSTEIN

In 1816, English novelist Mary Wollstonecraft Shelley wrote a book called *Frankenstein, or, The Modern Prometheus.* During this time in England, society was undergoing a change called the "Industrial Revolution." After thousands of years of farming, people were moving into cities, and creating machines that could do their work for them. Automatic looms were built that could weave clothes much faster than people could weave. Machines could pump water faster than people, and engines began to do factory work for the first time.

Below: A poster for the 1931 film *Frankenstein.*

Many people lost their jobs to the technological advances. People who ran the machines had to work in nightmarish factories. Factory owners treated their workers more like animals than human beings. It seemed that science and technology were moving at a breathtaking speed. What would come next? Would the future be wonderful, but only for machines? It seemed like a disaster for people. Mary Shelley wrote a novel that gave a possible answer to the question. *Frankenstein* was a tale of terror that many scholars say was the first true science fiction novel.

Shelley wrote *Frankenstein* when she was only 19 years old. She and her future husband, the famous English poet Percy Shelley, were staying in Switzerland with some friends. A long stretch of cold and dreary weather forced the group indoors, where they entertained themselves by reading ghost stories. One night they decided to have a contest to see who could write the scariest story.

Above: Mary Wollstonecraft Shelley at her writing desk.

Mary Shelley got her inspiration from a nightmare, in which she saw a troubled man kneeling beside a creature, a horror created by his own two hands. With this seed of an idea, Shelley feverishly wrote her novel.

The story is about a deranged scientist, Victor Frankenstein, who uses modern technology to create life. Wielding this godlike power, Frankenstein gathers dead body parts and weaves them together, then uses sparks of electricity to bring the creature to life:

Below: Boris Karloff as Frankenstein's monster.

It was on a dreary night of November, that I beheld the accomplishment of my toils. … It was already one in the morning; the rain pattered dismally against the panes, and my candle was nearly burnt out, when, by the glimmer of the half-extinguished light, I saw the dull yellow eye of the creature open; it breathed hard, and a convulsive motion agitated its limbs.

At first, the scientist is thrilled with his amazing accomplishment, but it isn't long before the creator recoils in horror at his creation. Disgusted and panic-stricken, Victor Frankenstein runs away. The creature, abandoned and unloved by everyone it meets, finally seeks revenge against the man who brought him to life.

Mary Shelley's writing was influenced by many sources, especially the Gothic, gloomy literature of her time. It's also possible that she suffered from depression. Further, she may have been grieving because she gave birth to a stillborn baby the year before. Whatever the cause, the nightmare vision that stirred her to write *Frankenstein* became one of the most popular stories of its time. More than two centuries later, writers and filmmakers continue to produce countless remakes and sequels.

People identify with *Frankenstein*'s main theme. It is a warning to humanity not to "overreach," not to blindly use new technology without understanding the consequences. Like any good science fiction story, *Frankenstein* is about an idea: science can do great harm when used in the blind pursuit of power.

Above: Victor Frankenstein, played by Colin Clive, realizes he has created a monster.

ROBOTS GONE WILD

Right: Robby the Robot.

Are robots helpful to humanity? Or are they ready to become murderous monsters at any minute? In some science fiction and horror stories, robots behave themselves. They do what they are supposed to do, which is to help, serve, and protect their human owners. Robby the Robot, from the 1956 film *Forbidden Planet,* was one of the first to always obey its masters. The bubble-headed robot from the 1960s TV series *Lost in Space* was always helpful. The robot always kept a watchful eye on Will Robinson, the youngest member of the family, and became a good friend to him. Whenever an intruder threatened, the robot was quick to sound the alarm: "Danger! Danger, Will Robinson!"

Of course, two of the most famous robots are C3PO and R2-D2 from the *Star Wars* movies. C3PO is funny and clumsy, and R2-D2 is stubborn and headstrong. But despite their personalities, they always work to serve humans. They are not only helpful and eager to please, they are even heroic. They frequently put themselves in danger in order to protect or serve their human owners.

However, for every nice robot, there is a mechanical menace lurking in the shadows. It's a common fear that mankind's technology will someday turn against us. One of the first movies to explore this topic was made in 1926. The movie was called *Metropolis,* directed by Fritz Lang. In *Metropolis,* an insane inventor creates an evil robot named Maria.

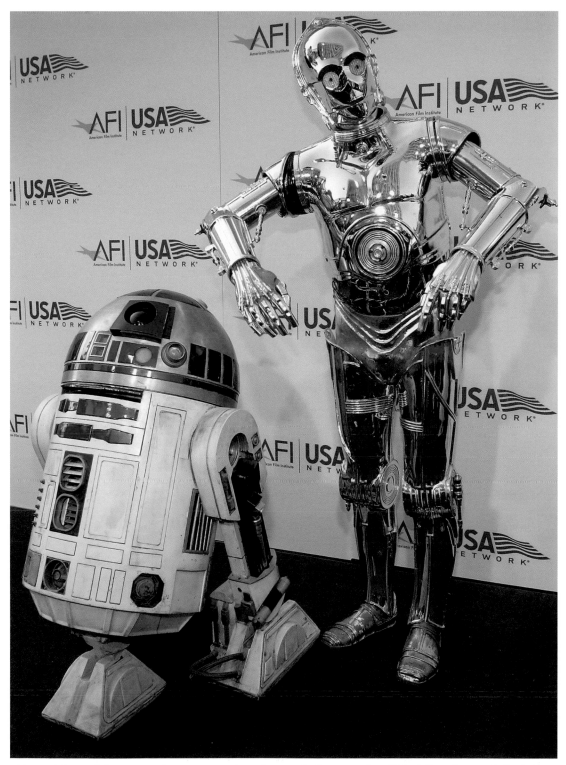

Above: Two of the most famous movie robots of all time, *Star Wars'* R2-D2 and C3PO.

Other such movies include *Futureworld*, released in 1976. In *Futureworld*, a group of robots plots to replace humans and take over the world. Ash is the name of the human-looking robot from the 1984 film *Alien*. Ash keeps a dark secret from his human companions.

In the film *2001: A Space Odyssey*, two astronauts must shut off the malfunctioning computer that controls their ship. The computer realizes that the astronauts are trying to shut it down, so it fights back. Finally, one of the astronauts crawls up inside the computer and pulls out its circuits. As the computer slowly loses its brain, it utters the famous line, "My mind is going... I can feel it..." But it begs a question: Can a computer really feel?

In the 1982 movie *Blade Runner*, a group of human-looking androids, called replicants, escapes. Humans see the replicants as a menace. Harrison Ford plays Deckard, a "blade runner" whose job is to hunt them down. Before their time runs out, the replicants try to contact their creator in an attempt to prolong their short lives. They try to survive—isn't that an important quality of being human?

Below: In 1982's *Blade Runner*, a replicant (Rutger Hauer) grabs Deckard (Harrison Ford), the man sent to hunt down all the replicants.

Above: Actor Will Smith starred in 2004's *I, Robot.*

The 2004 movie *I, Robot* stars Will Smith as a detective trying to solve a murder. He finds out that a group of evil robots is responsible. At least, it seems that way at first. He has to fight his own prejudices about robots to wrestle with the question, "When does a robot become human?"

As with all good science fiction and horror, movies like these give us a new way to look at ourselves. These stories can make us think. What does it mean to be human? Is it ethical to make a machine human-like, and then deny it freedom? What happens when the created try to destroy the creator? Is all life precious, even if it was created on a workbench? These stories can help us think about ourselves and our understanding of life.

MUTANTS

In 1945, at the end of World War II, the United States dropped atomic bombs on the Japanese cities of Hiroshima and Nagasaki. While those bombs ended the war, they caused a horrific loss of life and brought the world into the nuclear age. Even though scientists used the nuclear weapons, they did not understand them fully. They understood even less about nuclear power.

In the 1950s, another theme emerged in horror stories. Movies were made that reflected people's fears of atomic energy and toxic waste. These stories envisioned situations where scientists intentionally or accidentally meddled with nature.

The movie *Them* (1954) featured giant ants that were mutated due to underground nuclear explosions. The 1954 Japanese movie *Gojira* (Godzilla) was about a giant reptile awakened by nuclear testing. In 1955, the movie *Tarantula* featured a giant mutant spider. *The Deadly Mantis* (1957) was about an enormous, prehistoric praying mantis.

This category of movies remains popular even today, with examples such as the *Eight Legged Freaks* (2002), and the low-budget giant radioactive mosquito film, *Proboscis* (2000).

Below: A poster and images from 2002's *Eight Legged Freaks.*

Above: (top) A 1956 *Godzilla* poster and (bottom) an image from the 1998 *Godzilla* movie.

Above: Sam Neill as paleontologist Alan Grant in *Jurassic Park III*. *Below:* The original book *Jurassic Park* by Michael Crichton.

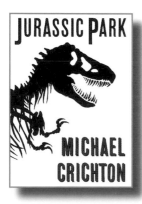

Another popular category of horror movie explores the dangers of genetic engineering. Genes are the basic building blocks of life, and scientists today are just beginning to understand them. Some scientists believe they will soon be able to control genes, such as turning off the bad genes that cause disease. It makes sense, then, that authors would write stories about genetic engineering gone bad.

One of the most popular movies about genetic engineering is *Jurassic Park* (1993), directed by Steven Spielberg and based on the 1990 book by Michael Crichton. In this movie, scientists find DNA (the building blocks of genes) of dinosaurs, and then clone them. This creates real-life dinosaurs. The scientists intend to build a theme park where people can come to see the dinosaurs. However, the dinosaurs refuse to be contained. As one of the main characters says, "Life will find a way." Scientists find themselves unable to predict what happens to the genetically engineered creatures, and disaster results. A theme of the movie, as with many movies of this type, is that some scientists believe they will never make a mistake. Their uncontrolled egos end up creating a disaster.

Resident Evil was a popular video game that was made into a 2002 movie. The story follows a similar theme. Scientists create a terrible virus. Unfortunately, the virus gets loose, killing hundreds of people and turning many into zombies and other creatures.

DOOM is another video game that was turned into a movie. It has the same theme, with a simple story line: 1) scientific meddling; 2) monsters are created; 3) send in people to kill the monsters.

Whether it be the atomic age of the 1950s, or genetic engineering today, stories reveal the things that make us afraid.

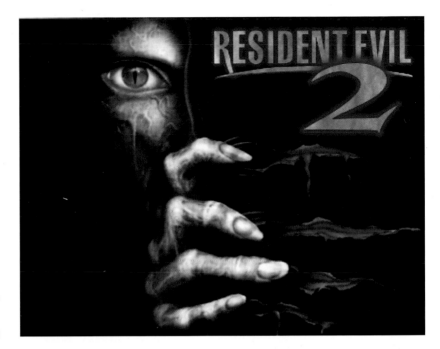

Above: Images from *Resident Evil 2* and *DOOM*.

Stories help us cope with our fear. They also give us a way to think through the issues that frighten us. These kinds of stories can, perhaps, bring humility before nature. In many of these movies, people think they can control everything about nature. However, nature is unpredictable. Nature doesn't always lend itself to being captured and controlled. In these movies, when scientists get overconfident, nature fights back.

TIME TRAVEL DANGER

I f a person could travel back in time, what might happen? Could the time traveler change the future? Might the time traveler create a disaster? That very thing happened in the 2005 movie *A Sound of Thunder*, which was based on the book by Ray Bradbury.

In the story, time traveling tourists go back in time to participate in a dinosaur safari. They are given strict orders to leave history undisturbed, because even a small change could have disastrous consequences for the future. The hunters must stay on a special path that hovers above the jungle floor, and can only shoot dinosaurs that are already about to die. However, one of the hunters accidentally steps on an insect. This tiny change alters history so much that the world is almost unrecognizable when the hunters return to their own time.

Below: Two time-travel movies that warn of the consequences that can occur when history is altered.

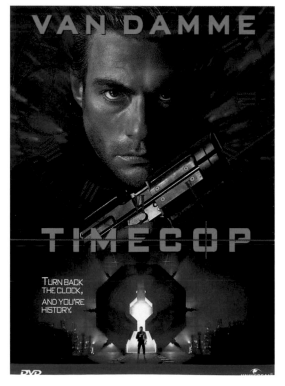

The 1994 movie *Timecop* featured a special police force that protected the world by keeping people from going back in time to change events. The 2003 sequel, *Timecop 2: The Berlin Decision*, followed a few people who went back in time to try to kill Adolf Hitler before he became the Nazi leader of World War II. The timecop had a decision to make. Should he follow his orders and protect the timeline? Or allow the worst dictator in history to be killed before he actually murdered anyone?

Above: Author Ray Bradbury with some of his science fiction toys.

Above: Arnold Schwarzenegger played the killer robot in 1984's *The Terminator*.

Perhaps the most frightening example of a time-travel disaster is shown in the 1984 movie *The Terminator*. In the future, there is a terrible war between machines and humanity. The humans finally win the war, but the machines send back a robot to kill the mother of John Conner, the man who led humanity to victory. The unstoppable robot assassin tries hard to change the future. In addition, the robots try to change the future for two more sequels.

Time travel is a fun topic. It's always interesting to think about how things might be different. Perhaps these kinds of movies help us to think about how our actions today affect our future tomorrow.

Above: The killer robot from *The Terminator*, sent back in time to change the future.

Dr. Jekyll and Mr. Hyde

In 1886, Robert Louis Stevenson wrote a short novel titled *The Strange Case of Dr. Jekyll and Mr. Hyde*. Like *Frankenstein*, the book was destined to become a classic, repeated in many movies and stories to come. Stevenson wrote the novel in the "first person," which means that it reads as if Dr. Jekyll himself wrote the words.

Dr. Jekyll was a friendly scientist who created a potion that turned him into a terrible, ugly man called Mr. Hyde. At first, Dr. Jekyll liked the idea of becoming Mr. Hyde, who could do terrible things that Dr. Jekyll would never do. However, Mr. Hyde was a brute who didn't feel bad about injuring people or even killing them. Soon, Dr. Jekyll decided never to take the mysterious potion again. However, the good doctor began to change into Mr. Hyde even without the potion. He realizes that Mr. Hyde is taking over, and is afraid that he will soon become Mr. Hyde permanently. In the last part of the book, Dr. Jekyll fearfully says that he may never return from being the evil Mr. Hyde.

Above Right: An image from *Dr. Jekyll and Mr. Hyde.* *Below:* A poster from the 1931 film starring Fredric March.

Robert Louis Stevenson wrote a story about an experiment that went awry, but it was really about the struggle between good and evil. Sometimes, good and evil are a part of the same person. We sometimes do good things, and we sometimes do bad things, and this is what Stevenson was trying to explore. In this story of a medical experiment gone bad, we see a normal person become wildly irrational.

Even today, people who behave normally sometimes, and irrationally other times, are sometimes described as a "Dr. Jekyll and Mr. Hyde."

Above: Author Robert Lewis Stevenson wrote the original story *The Strange Case of Dr. Jekyll and Mr. Hyde.*

SLASHERS AND SPLATTERS

A common type of movie today is called the "slasher film." This is a category of horror film where brutal murderers stalk and violently kill their victims. The killings are unprovoked, with no reason behind them. The only motivation to kill is for the sake of killing. These kinds of movies are sometimes called "splatter movies" because the directors use gallons of red liquid that splatters everywhere when people are killed.

One of the first slasher films was *Halloween*, directed by John Carpenter in 1978. It showed an unstoppable psycho-killer, murdering and scaring people. It produced many sequels.

One of the most famous characters in slasher movies is Jason, from the series of movies begun in 1980 titled *Friday the 13th*. Jason started out as a deformed child, and other children made fun of him. The abuse he took from his parents, guardians, and other children made him into a terrible killer. He is famous as the man behind the hockey mask, holding a large knife or a chainsaw. He stalked his victims, usually teenagers in isolated areas. As the movie sequels continued, he took on a supernatural quality.

Below: Two famous slasher characters come together in 2003's *Freddy vs Jason.*

Another movie to take advantage of the popular slasher film theme was *Nightmare on Elm Street* in 1984. Again, the movie produced many sequels. This series featured the character Freddy Krueger, who has supernatural abilities. He has the power to invade people's dreams. True to the slasher genre, he stalks and kills many innocent people.

Directors like to make these movies because they can be made very inexpensively. Some critics say these movies glorify violence and killing. Others say these movies explore the evil that is around us. Others say they simply entertain people who want a cheap scare.

Above: Director John Carpenter has created several horror films, including *Halloween* and its many sequels.

JACK THE RIPPER

Are there real slasher stories? Unfortunately, yes. Sometimes, these man-made horror stories are indeed true. One of the most famous real-life horrors is Jack the Ripper. He was one of the first widely publicized serial killers—someone who kills several people over a short period of time.

"Jack" wasn't his real name. In fact, we don't know what his real name was, because police never caught him. It might have been the newspapers that gave him the name, "Jack the Ripper." It gave the killer an instantly recognizable title—and it was a way to sell more newspapers.

The year was 1888, in London, England. On August 25, a young woman was brutally murdered, and then mutilated with a knife. Over the next few months, four other women were killed in the same way.

The panic that gripped the city caused a massive increase in newspaper sales. People wanted to read everything they could about the killer. This is one of the reasons why Jack the Ripper is so famous. He wasn't the first serial killer, and unfortunately, wasn't the last. But he killed at a time when the newspapers were just getting started, and so his killings were the first ones that were widely publicized and read.

Police searched valiantly for the killer, but their techniques were not very good in those days. They didn't study or come to understand the criminal mind. They couldn't read fingerprints, and didn't have DNA analysis.

Below: The front page of a September 1888 newspaper.

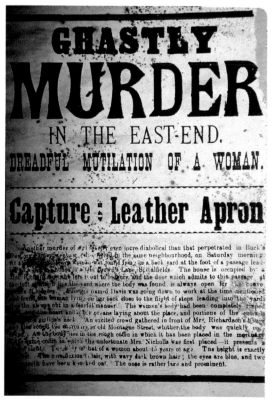

Because of poor police records, historians and modern detectives are not even sure how many people Jack the Ripper actually killed. There were probably at least five women killed, but possibly several more. There were many accusations and theories about who the murderer was. The fact that several of the victims had internal organs removed led some people to believe that the killer had some medical experience, and could even have been a doctor.

In a few of the murders, the police discovered the victim within minutes of the killing. They had a number of suspects, but no one was ever arrested. Finally, the murders simply stopped. To this day, the identity of Jack the Ripper remains a mystery.

Above: A photo of a street in east London where the body of one of Jack the Ripper's victims was found.

REAL-LIFE HORRORS

esides Jack the Ripper, are there any real, man-made horrors today? Unfortunately, the answer is yes. Many animal species are quickly becoming extinct, due mostly to our destruction of the animals' habitat. Pollution creates toxic areas. Overuse of pesticide kills fish in rivers.

Then there are technological disasters. In 1986, part of a nuclear power plant in Eastern Europe exploded. The plant is located in the town of Chernobyl, in what is today the country of Ukraine. The escaped radiation poisoned hundreds of square miles of land, which will remain toxic for hundreds of years. Even today, birth defects and cancer are much higher in the area near Chernobyl.

Right: Alehandra Lihova, the sister of a worker who died following the clean-up operations of the 1986 Chernobyl nuclear explosion, cries at the April 26, 2004, wreath-laying ceremony at the Chernobyl victim monument in Kiev, Ukraine. Chernobyl is considered the world's worst nuclear disaster.

ІЗ МОГИЛОЮ ПОРУЧ
І ПОБІЛЯ ЧАЕС
БІЛЯ МЕРТВОЇ ПРИП'ЯТІ -

Above: Heavy smog from vehicles and industry covers the city of Los Angeles, CA.

Global warming is a soon-to-be man-made horror. We have polluted the environment and overused natural resources, and the result will be a world that heats up. The increased heat will create more extreme weather, more droughts, and more problems for people, unless something is done to reverse the damage.

Good stories give us hope, give us courage, and give us warnings. Good stories will help us think about difficult issues. Stories can help us to plan a better future. Stories can also warn us about the dangers of science and technology. When we use science and technology without thinking of the consequences of what we are doing, then we are bound to create new problems.

The world needs kids who grow up to be scientists who think before they act. We need scientists who understand that science and technology can either harm us or help us. These future scientists need to respect nature, and make the decisions that will help humanity.

Above: The high-mileage, gas/electric-powered Toyota Prius decreases air pollution. *Below:* A plastic recycling plant. The small pellets are reused to make plastic bottles.

GLOSSARY

ANDROID

A kind of robot that mimics people, both in appearance and behavior. In the film *Blade Runner*, replicants are a type of android.

CLONE

An organism that is "grown" from donor cells, making an exact copy of the original.

GOTHIC

A type of literature, which was especially popular in the late 18th and 19th centuries, that uses remote settings and sinister atmosphere to suggest horror and mystery. Mary Wollstonecraft Shelley was heavily influenced by the Gothic style of literature when she wrote *Frankenstein* in 1816.

INDUSTRIAL REVOLUTION

The rapid development of industry that happened in the late 18th and early 19th centuries, especially in Great Britain and other Western countries. The Industrial Revolution is usually characterized by steam power, the growth of factories, and mass-manufactured goods. Science fiction became popular as science and manufacturing became more and more important in people's lives.

PROMETHEUS

Prometheus was a Greek demigod, one of the Titans, who stole fire from Zeus in heaven and brought it back to Earth to benefit mankind. As punishment, Zeus had Prometheus chained to a rock, where a vulture came each day to eat the demigod's liver, which grew back every night. Prometheus was eventually rescued by Hercules. When Mary Shelley named her novel, *Frankenstein, or, the Modern Prometheus*, she meant that Dr. Frankenstein, like all of mankind, can do great harm in the blind pursuit of power.

SCIENCE FICTION

Hard science fiction emphasizes facts and reality. It is filled with scientific detail and presents a realistic speculation of how science will affect future societies. Soft science fiction emphasizes plot and characters more than scientific detail and realism. The *Star Wars* movies are often considered soft science fiction. For example, space battles in *Star Wars* feature noisy and fiery explosions, impossible in the airless vacuum of space.

WORLD WAR II

A war that was fought from 1939 to 1945, involving countries around the world. The United States entered the war after Japan's bombing of the American naval base at Pearl Harbor, in Oahu, Hawaii, on December 7, 1941.

Above: Director Steven Spielberg with his man-made dinosaur creation from *Jurassic Park*.

INDEX

Above: A poster from *The Phantom Creeps.*